Using Digital Games as Assessment and Instruction Tools

Ryan L. Schaaf

Solution Tree | Press

a division of
Solution Tree

555 North Morton Street
Bloomington, IN 47404
800.733.6786 (toll free) / 812.336.7700
FAX: 812.336.7790
email: info@solution-tree.com
solution-tree.com

Visit **go.solution-tree.com/technology** to access materials related to this book.

Printed in the United States of America

19 18 17 16 15   1 2 3 4 5

FSC
www.fsc.org
MIX
Paper from
responsible sources
FSC® C011935

Library of Congress Cataloging-in-Publication Data

Schaaf, Ryan L.
  Using digital games as assessment and instruction tools / Ryan L. Schaaf.
     pages cm. -- (Solutions)
  Includes bibliographical references.
  ISBN 978-1-935542-53-7 (perfect bound) 1. Educational games. 2. Simulation games in education. 3. Education (Elementary)--Computer-assisted instruction. 4. Education (Secondary)--Computer-assisted instruction. I. Title.
  LB1029.G3S35 2015
  371.33'7--dc23
                              2015007947

Solution Tree
Jeffrey C. Jones, CEO
Edmund M. Ackerman, President

Solution Tree Press
President: Douglas M. Rife
Associate Acquisitions Editor: Kari Gillesse
Editorial Director: Lesley Bolton
Managing Production Editor: Caroline Weiss
Copy Editor: Ashante K. Thomas
Text and Cover Designer: Rian Anderson

I dedicate this book to my beautiful wife, Rachel. Thank you for helping me fulfill my dreams and conquer life's challenges. To my loving boys—grow up into good men who treat people with dignity and respect. To my family and friends—thank you for sticking with me through my battle with cancer. To Ian, Nicky, and Notre Dame of Maryland University—thank you for helping me grow as a professional in the academic realm. I would like to thank the Solution Tree team for its help with this project, specifically Jeff Jones, Edmund Ackerman, Douglas Rife, Kari Gillesse, Ashante Thomas, Rian Anderson, and Jessi Finn.

Acknowledgments

I would like to acknowledge the support of InfoSavvy21 in this unique endeavor. In regards to the Digital Learning Game Database (DLGD), I would like to acknowledge Devin DeLange and her hard work assisting me with creating a great resource for educators interested in incorporating digital gaming into instruction.

Visit **go.solution-tree.com/technology** to access materials related to this book.

Table of Contents

About the Author..**xi**

Introduction: The Gamer in All of Us......................**1**
    From Entertainment to Edutainment to Education 3
    Teachers Versus Facilitators..................................8

**Chapter 1: Finding Good Digital Games—Where
to Look** **11**
    Web Browser–Based Games..................................12
        Sheppard Software 12
        PBS KIDS Games 12
        Mr. Nussbaum 13
        National Geographic Kids 13
        Poptropica 13
        Funbrain 13
        PrimaryGames 14
        ABCya.com 14
        Arcademic Skill Builders 14
        Games for Change 14
        PowerMyLearning 14
        The Stacks 15
    Facilitate Gaming Experiences With Browser-Based Games..15
    Steam 16
    Gaming Consoles..17

App Markets: Tablets and Smartphones 19

    The Oregon Trail: American Settler.........................20

    Angry Birds 20

    VocabularySpellingCity 21

    DragonBox Algebra 5+ 21

    Powers of Minus Ten....................................21

    ThinkerToy: Shapes.....................................21

    Math Duel: 2 Player Math Game.........................21

    Bridge Constructor......................................22

The Most Popular Strategy for Finding Digital Games 22

Chapter 2: Evaluating and Field Testing Digital Games . 25

Learning With Digital Games: Strategies That Work 29

    Lesson Motivation 30

    Free Play 31

    Baseline to Finish Line...................................32

    Setting a Mental Stage 33

    Gaming With Anticipation................................34

    Teams and Tournaments.................................35

    A Learning Event 36

The "Long Experience" of Playing and Learning 37

    Minecraft and *MinecraftEdu*...............................38

    The Sandbox and *The Sandbox EDU*.....................38

    WoW in School 39

    Lure of the Labyrinth 39

Chapter 3: Gaming and Instructional Assessment 41

Summative Assessment....................................42

Repetition: Test-Taking Preparation and Review..............44

Formative Assessment 45

Stealth Assessment 46

Learning Analytics 47

Takeaways for Readers 49

    Takeaway 1: Five Educational Super Blogs for Digital Learning. . 49

Takeaway 2: *Evernote* Public Notebook 51
Takeaway 3: Digital Learning Game Database 51
Takeaway 4: DLGD Participation 51
Leveling Up Classrooms 52

Appendix: Discussion Questions **55**

References and Resources **57**

About the Author

 **Ryan L. Schaaf** is the assistant professor of educational technology at Notre Dame of Maryland University and a faculty associate for the Johns Hopkins University School of Education graduate program—the same program he graduated from with a master of science in instructional technology and technology leadership in schools. With over fifteen years in the education field, Ryan has been a teacher, instructional leader, curriculum designer, and technology integration specialist in Howard County, Maryland. In 2007, he was nominated for Maryland Teacher of the Year.

Ryan has published numerous research articles related to the use of digital games as an effective instructional strategy in the classroom in *New Horizons for Learning* and *The Canadian Journal of Action Research*.

Ryan is developing and instructing face-to-face, hybrid, and online courses for both Notre Dame of Maryland University and Johns Hopkins. His passion is presenting sessions and keynotes about the potential for gaming in the classroom, the characteristics of 21st century learning, and emerging technologies and trends in education.

His books include *Making School a Game Worth Playing: Digital Games in the Classroom* and *Reinventing Learning for the Always-On Generation: Strategies and Apps That Work.*

Ryan is happily married to his beautiful wife, Rachel, and has two little boys who are his pride and joy. In his free time, he enjoys fishing, exercising, gardening, and volunteering in local schools. To learn more about Ryan's work, follow @RyanLSchaaf on Twitter.

To book Ryan L. Schaaf for professional development, contact pd@solution-tree.com.

Introduction:
The Gamer in All of Us

My seven-year-old son loves to play digital games! Whether on a gaming console or tablet, he enjoys this form of entertainment the most. Although he enjoys reading books, watching movies, and researching using the web, the interactive nature of a video game draws him in. He is proud of his accomplishments during gameplay. My little man boasts about upgrading his characters or unlocking a new tool during gameplay with as much of a sense of pride and accomplishment as he would have for scoring a touchdown in his football game, getting an "A" on his spelling test, or catching a fish. It takes a great deal of work, time, strategy, and commitment to achieve goals during gameplay—perhaps as much as it does to score a touchdown or earn an A on a test. Despite the constant time and mental energy he sacrifices in the pursuit of virtual fame and fortune, my son has fun—deep fun! This book explores what happens when hard work is paired with deep fun; it will help solve the following equation: Hard Work + Deep Fun = ?.

My son is not alone. Young Cordell Steiner, a third-grade student from Minnesota, makes a passionate plea in a TEDx conference for teachers to use digital games in their classrooms for teaching, learning, and assessment (Steiner, 2014). He speaks of the benefits of individualized learning—learning specifically focused on the particular needs of a student. For instance, if a student must learn or review geometric angles, then he or she plays a game where the concept is explored in a highly immersive and interactive manner with immediate feedback. Cordell also conveys the point that games allow players to fail and try again. In traditional forms of classroom assessment, this type of failure is often rewarded with a low grade. If a player fails in a digital game, then the player clicks the reset button (in the game and on the learning process). Truth be told, digital games have a lot to teach our students and a great deal to teach educators about learning and assessment during the digital age.

My son and Cordell are growing up surrounded by digital games. The global video game industry is big business. With projected global revenue of over $80 billion a year, the gaming industry is attracting new users every day. As of 2013, more than 1.2 billion people play some form of digital game. Ninety-one percent of U.S. children between the ages of two and seventeen play video games as of 2011 (NPD Group, 2011).

If the results focus only on teens, then "97% play computer, web, portable, or console games" as indicated by Lenhart et al. (2008) in a Pew Research Center's Internet and American Life Project survey. Of these teenage video game players, 99 percent of the boys and 94 percent of the girls surveyed said they played some form of video game (Lenhart et al., 2008). Although male players outnumbered female players in 2008, this demographic is quickly changing. When comparing the gender of game players, women over the age of thirty-five outnumber men. This trend in data is quickly changing the preconceived notion that digital games are played only by male teens in isolated, dark basements at all hours of the night. More and more people from all walks of life are picking up a controller, downloading an app, or logging into these imaginative worlds for entertainment.

The popularity of gaming has not gone unnoticed. Corporate powerhouses such as McDonald's, Nike, and Starbucks use elements of games to bolster their customer loyalty programs and boost sales

(Chou, 2013). Other companies such as Cold Stone Creamery, the Miller Brewing Company, Bank of America, Marriott, Canon, Pfizer, and Cisco Systems use digital games or simulations to train their employees in skills involving human resources, customer service, or professional development (Entertainment Software Association, 2014; Kane & Meyers, 2010; Malhoit, 2012; University of Colorado Denver, 2010). Even the military, which is grounded in decades of tradition and is very particular in how it trains its recruits, uses digital games as recruiting and training tools. Video games have become ubiquitous in today's digital culture.

Gaming's next logical step is to integrate into the field of education. Although in the past digital games were adopted sparsely in small pockets of classrooms, the meteoric rise of gaming's mainstream popularity and appeal has caused educators to take another serious look at digital games as tools and learning environments for deep, fun, and engaging learning.

From Entertainment to Edutainment to Education

Playing digital games is a popular form of entertainment—this is a fairly safe assumption to make. Simple real-world observations attest to gaming's connection to our youth. Go to a restaurant such as Buffalo Wild Wings, and the restaurant passes out tablets for its patrons' children to use. On each tablet (besides germs and barbeque sauce) are digital games ready to engage children in gameplay, allowing their parents to have a conversation that doesn't involve children's television shows like *Barney* or *Teletubbies*. This recurring pattern of turning over mobile devices to children is occurring elsewhere. A quick scan at restaurants, in the backseats of cars, or in homes draws a simple, crystal-clear conclusion—our youth love to ingest media: "Seventy-two percent of children age 8 and under have used a mobile device for some type of media activity such as playing games, watching videos, or using apps" (Rideout, 2013). These children, the members of the always-on generation, are growing up with hundreds of ways to consume and produce information using media.

The members of the digital generation do not believe they live two separate lives, one digital and one real. They exist in both worlds simultaneously—a form of hybrid consciousness. According to Catherine Beavis (2012), "Popular culture and the digital world are an important part of many children's lives. Computer games, virtual worlds and social networking sites are seamlessly integrated into their everyday work, relationships and play"(p. 17). What the digital generation learns and experiences digitally is just as relevant to these learners as their real-world experiences.

The adults in charge of the always-on generation must understand that these students learn differently and use different tools and approaches to accomplish their academic growth. In previous generations, there were three ways to communicate with friends—by telephone, via mail, or in person. In today's world, the digital world, the digital generation has hundreds of ways to connect with friends. In the past, students consulted encyclopedias to search for information. Today, this generation uses Siri, Wikipedia, and Google to find facts and resources for its research. Previous generations of children were free to play outside from dawn until dusk with little to no adult supervision. Nowadays, the fear of predators has forced more and more children into their homes. They are not allowed to loiter at shopping malls or after school, so they connect digitally. The digital generation plays video games, watches and records YouTube videos, and shares its life experiences using social networks such as Twitter, Instagram, and Snapchat.

In addition, these generations of children are far from being the first to flock to media at such a young age. After fifty triumphant years of entertaining children, Saturday morning cartoons are no more. Children simply don't want to settle for a single morning a week of media programmed especially for them. Interactive media forms (such as digital games) are like brain candy to the digital generation and provide colorful, high-quality, highly expressive, and realistic graphics for them to ingest at their convenience. Although media like television, books, pictures, and music have an important role in communicating information, to some extent, interaction with these media can be a one-way street. Now this is not an assault on television, books, pictures, and music. They are still powerful forms of communication. However, in most cases viewers cannot alter a story line, change music lyrics, or change a static image. In digital games, the player controls the story line, characters, and outcomes in the game—giving young gamers a sense of ownership for the first time in their lives.

Using digital games to teach students is not a new endeavor. Edutainment is the process of educating through the use of popular forms of entertainment. In the 1980s, students were introduced to the first desktop computers. The Apple IIc introduced students to *The Oregon Trail*, *Number Munchers*, and *Where in the World Is Carmen Sandiego?* Despite the fun and excitement of these early learning games, many students failed to make the connection to what each game or tool was trying to convey to them. The main reason for this: teachers didn't know how to implement these tools for deep, immersive learning. First, they lacked extensive training. The computers and games looked intriguing. Students would practice basic mathematics facts or explore geography and history, but once the game was over, where did it fit into the classroom? Many teachers let students play in isolation to keep students occupied during non-instructional filler time. Next, classrooms lacked enough computer workstations to attempt a widespread integration effort. Computers were very expensive and were purchased by schools over an extended period of time. Finally, there was a lack of game inventory to choose from—learning video games were still in their infancy, so there were slim pickings for teachers. These reasons relegated these early video games to the role of edutainment or fun digital centers to visit after students' "real" work was completed.

As computer hardware and digital technologies evolved, digital learning games became more relevant to students, teachers, and parents. Many factors added to this newfound relevance involving gaming and learning. First, the prices for computers and mobile devices have decreased tremendously. Schools and parents now have the capability to buy desktop computers, laptops, tablets, or smartphones. Next, there is a wider range and variety of digital learning games to choose from. Every age level, every content area, and every technological platform now has an extensive catalog of games for purchase or download. Finally, other forms of nontraditional educational media such as video, social media, and web-based tools are more widely adopted and used at home and in schools. Parents would much rather have their kids play and learn on PBS KIDS online than another website they deem noneducational. In schools, educators are adopting new tools to teach with every day. Years ago, showing a YouTube video to a class would have been considered taboo. Nowadays, many educators are seeing the value of using video content to enrich their daily lessons. The times and tools in today's classroom have changed.

Traditional educational theorists such as Jean Piaget, John Dewey, Immanuel Kant, and Friedrich Fröebel indicate the power of play in childhood development and learning (Huang & Plass, 2009). As we fast-forward to the age of computers and the creation of the new digital landscape, the forms of play have evolved and multiplied extensively (although the old ways still work). The members of the digital generation play video games for fun *and* experience powerful learning in the virtual worlds they are immersed in. In these digital spaces, students are provided opportunities to learn through failure, take control of their actions, collaborate, and achieve goals with constant praise and reward. In many of these games and virtual worlds, there are opportunities to learn new content and explore new concepts.

Mathematician, computer scientist, and educator Seymour Papert helps link the educational theories of the past to the practices educators are using in today's classrooms. He was perhaps the first "concerned with digital tools and children. His awareness that children effectively think differently than adults, and that their cognitive evolution requires designing rich toolkits and environments rather than force-feeding knowledge, has set the tone for decades of research" (Blikstein, 2013). Many digital games provide these rich toolkits and environments Papert refers to.

More and more teachers are using digital games in the classroom (Takeuchi & Vaala, 2014). The Cooney Center survey, which interviewed almost seven hundred K–8 teachers, focuses on understanding the ways teachers are using digital games in the classroom. Over 75 percent of teachers surveyed report using digital games in their classrooms. That is an increase of over 25 percent since 2012. "Teachers say they want to use digital games to deliver standards-based content and assess student knowledge and skills," says Cooney Center's senior director and research scientist (and survey designer) Lori Takeuchi. "But they're mixed on how effective games have been in doing these things" (Korbey, 2014).

Alas, this struggle is a popular one when integrating digital games into classrooms. Teachers are under the preconceived notion that teaching has to be standard in a standards-based curriculum. Nothing is further from the truth. Although academic standards dictate what knowledge or skills educators must help engrain into their students, the strategies and methods at the educators' disposal are *not* mandated. Using a fun, immersive, and engaging medium such as digital gaming invigorates lessons while still addressing Common Core State Standards or state, district, or local content standards.

This text helps educators integrate digital games into K–12 lessons. In chapter 1, readers uncover potential video games by exploring the numerous outlets and platforms they can search through. By chapter 2, readers first learn how to evaluate digital games for potential use then gain numerous instructional strategies to use with students. Next, chapter 3 introduces the idea of using digital games as summative and formative assessment tools for valuable insights into student performance. Finally, this text offers readers numerous takeaways for educators that are indoctrinated into using digital games for teaching and assessment. *Using Digital Games as Assessment and Instruction Tools* provides an easy-to-use resource for locating games to incorporate into lessons based on the content of the game. Dozens of assessment and instructional strategies are introduced and summarized for easy replication in classrooms of all grade levels. Readers will be able to participate in curating effective digital games for other educators to use in their classrooms.

Teachers Versus Facilitators

Throughout this text, the term *teacher* is used less and less. It will be replaced with the term *facilitator*. This isn't an insult to teachers or their time-honored profession—it is just a term that better describes what role an educator assumes when utilizing digital game–based learning (DGBL). In traditional classroom settings, the teacher is the ultimate source of information. However, using games as instructional tools takes the focus off of teachers to provide information to students. In this learning approach, students use digital games as tools and virtual environments to explore new concepts and learn new information. In DGBL, students become the star and center of their own learning.

> Game-based learning promotes a student-centered approach to instruction. Digital games allow teachers to step out of the spotlight during instruction and become guides in the classroom, rather than the source

of all information. Students today prefer not to be lec-
tured at, or to receive information from one source.
They prefer to generate their own knowledge from
the readily available resources (digital and human)
around them. Students prefer participatory, collaborative learning communities in which the teacher
assumes the role of facilitator or guide to help students as needed, to steer them when necessary, and
to provide them with the resources and means to
solve problems. (Schaaf & Mohan, 2014, p. 8)

Some educators might fear that the teaching profession will be
replaced by digital technologies. The truth is the new tools and
approaches teachers use to facilitate learning for their students
will merely transform their role in classrooms. Change can be
a scary ordeal, especially for educators who have taught for over
ten, fifteen, or even twenty years and are comfortable with their
teaching style: "Under these circumstances, an effective approach is
to begin by starting small and selecting one lesson. By easing into
this model, teachers can learn how to adopt a potentially powerful,
appealing, and effective approach to learning" (Schaaf & Mohan,
2014, p. 8).

Educators must remember that Rome wasn't built in a day. With
practice, experimentation, and patience, new teaching approaches
can reinvigorate the learning process for educators and students
alike.

Chapter 1

Finding Good Digital Games: Where to Look

Finding good learning games is a task that requires research, time, and a bit of luck. The first key to finding a potential video game for learning is to understand how the game will be disseminated to the students. For example, if students do not have portable game consoles such as the Nintendo DS or a LeapPad, then games used for these types of devices will not work. Educators must think of the devices and technology infrastructure they have access to. If teachers have access to a cart filled with iPads, then that is the device they must specifically focus their game search on. Next, digital game–based facilitators must consider how the gameplay will occur with the students. Will each student have access to a device for the whole gaming experience? Will students need to break into small groups to share a device for gameplay? These logistical considerations are crucial factors for facilitators to consider when selecting a gaming platform students will use during the DGBL activity. The following are several different gaming platforms a learning facilitator might consider using with his or her students. Each type of gaming platform has positive and negative aspects to consider before engaging and funding a large-scale DGBL initiative.

Web Browser–Based Games

There are thousands of free, ready-to-play digital games available online at this very moment. With the use of a web browser such as Google Chrome, Mozilla Firefox, Safari, or Internet Explorer, educators are a web search away from finding content-specific games for their lessons. For instance, as a demonstration, imagine a mathematics class that is studying probability. A facilitator simply conducts a Google search using a query such as "Interactive probability game for kids" to find thousands of potential games for students to use. Since many schools already have an abundant supply of computers, this platform of digital game is the easiest to adopt into classrooms.

There are also the large, popular collections of digital games often referred to as *game hubs*. These sites house many different types of digital games tailored to many different ages as well as content areas.

Sheppard Software

Sheppard Software (www.sheppardsoftware.com) hosts hundreds of free, online educational games. The site organizes its games into categories, which allows players to easily navigate by subject area to find suitable games that cater to either an instructional need or a student's sense of curiosity and challenge. Sheppard Software provides resources for all grades preK to 12.

PBS KIDS Games

PBS KIDS (http://pbskids.org/games) creates curriculum-based entertainment. The site hosts a number of browser-based gaming experiences based on popular literary and media franchises such as *The Cat in the Hat, Curious George, Sesame Street,* and more. Games are organized by subject type, which includes mathematics, healthy habits, science, reading, and teamwork.

Mr. Nussbaum

Greg Nussbaum, a Virginia public school teacher, created Mr. Nussbaum (www.mrnussbaum.com), which has over 3,500 content pages with a wide variety of learning games organized by content type and grade level. This site is also optimized for use on a tablet and an interactive whiteboard, and is geared toward learners in grades preK to 8.

National Geographic Kids

Visit National Geographic Kids (http://kids.nationalgeographic .com/games) for over one hundred fun, engaging, and interactive science, action, adventure, geography, quiz, and puzzle games. For a free game hub, the production quality on games and interactives is amazing.

Poptropica

Poptropica (www.poptropica.com) is a virtual world that offers engaging quests, stories, and games. Players are immersed into an online environment rich in storytelling, problem solving, collaboration, competition, and literacy.

Funbrain

Funbrain (www.funbrain.com), created for preK through eighth-grade students, offers more than one hundred fun, interactive games that develop skills in mathematics, reading, and literacy. Players can also read a variety of popular books and comics on the site, including *Diary of a Wimpy Kid, Amelia Writes Again,* and *Brewster Rockit.*

PrimaryGames

With games and activities that meet curriculum needs for mathematics, science, language arts, and social studies, PrimaryGames (www.primarygames.com/games.php) houses over one thousand game titles. The site includes curriculum guides for teachers to use in conjunction with the games.

ABCya.com

This game site offers teacher-created and approved educational computer games for elementary students to learn mathematics and language arts on the web. ABCya.com (www.abcya.com) has been featured by the *New York Times*, Apple, and Fox News Channel and provides young students well-crafted games and activities.

Arcademic Skill Builders

Arcademic Skill Builders (www.arcademics.com/games) provides online educational video games that offer a powerful approach to learning basic mathematics, language arts, vocabulary, and thinking skills. Arcademic games challenge grade 1–6 students to improve their scores through repetitive, timed learning drills that provide immediate feedback.

Games for Change

Games for Change (2015) (www.gamesforchange.org) offers games for ages seven and up, and "facilitates the creation and distribution of social-impact games that serve as critical tools in humanitarian and educational efforts."

PowerMyLearning

PowerMyLearning (http://powermylearning.org) is the destination to find and use carefully curated K–12 academic games, videos, and interactives aligned to the Common Core State Standards and across a range of subjects like mathematics, English language arts, science, social studies, technology, and more.

The Stacks

One of the largest publishers of educational children's books, Scholastic, houses a large assortment of education games in a section known as "The Stacks" (www.scholastic.com/kids/stacks/games). Players visiting this hub will enjoy challenging games exploring literacy, writing, trivia, and puzzles.

Facilitate Gaming Experiences With Browser-Based Games

Facilitating a gaming experience with web browser–based games is easy to implement in the classroom. Web browser–based games are a fun and engaging option to offer to students and parents for support and extra practice at home. In the classroom setting, if students have access to their own desktop or laptop computer, then they can play simultaneously in a one-on-one computing environment. If there are more students than computer stations, then teachers can employ collaborative-gaming experiences with students. In this team-based learning environment, it is essential to give each team member a role during gameplay since everyone cannot play at the same time. Some of these learning roles can include coaches to offer advice to the player, questioners to connect the gameplay to what students are learning through a series of questions, scribes to record what the player is doing and saying, and group leaders to keep track of time and ensure the members of the group are adhering to their assigned roles. If the ratio of computers to students is high, then using digital games as learning centers is a viable option. In the past, this was the ideal classroom situation for using learning games in schools. The only consequence of this strategy is the tendency for teachers to let students play freely without observing their progress, checking for struggling students, or monitoring if a certain game is too easy for a player. In essence, the games become a digital babysitter if there is no instructional guidance or student accountability. A remedy for this predicament is for teachers to monitor student progress, assign gaming partners, or have students complete an exit ticket, self-evaluation, or assessment.

As gaming technologies evolve, game developers are finding new and improved ways to distribute game titles to consumers. One web-based distribution option that is gaining popularity is Steam.

Steam

Steam (http://store.steampowered.com) is the world's largest online-gaming platform. Steam's massive online catalog of over 3,500 games is available on PC, Mac, and Linux-based computers, mobile devices, and even smart televisions. With over forty million active community members, Steam has evolved into an online social-gaming haven. Gamers are able to enjoy gameplay, discuss strategy, develop helpful tutorials and reference pages, and share experiences and ratings through social media.

Although the main purpose of Steam is entertainment, there are numerous titles that are educational. There are typing games such as *Mavis Beacon Teaches Typing*, historical strategy games such as *Sid Meier's Civilization*, and literacy games such as *Squirt's Adventure*. Steam's easy-to-navigate interface includes helpful information to research such as what platform the game is available on (PC, Mac, Linux, or through the online Steam Play experience), customer reviews, game descriptions, and system requirements.

Steam is a platform that can easily provide a plethora of game choices for teachers to consider when preparing a DGBL experience. Steam in the classroom is similar to web browser–based games. Learning gamers must have access to a computer with web connectivity for it to work.

Gaming Consoles

It may be a stretch to envision a classroom having one or more gaming consoles for teachers and students to use as learning tools or as a connection to virtual learning environments. However, the truth is a significant portion of teachers using digital games in the classroom are starting to see the benefits of using these types of games with their students. In *Level Up Learning: A National Survey on Teaching With Digital Games*, a survey the Cooney Center conducted to examine how teachers and students use digital games in the classroom, results show that about 13 percent of students accessed digital games using a game console or handheld-gaming device—a significant niche in classrooms participating in DGBL experiences (Takeuchi & Vaala, 2014). Teachers must reimagine the purpose of gaming consoles and use them as instructional workstations, not entertainment systems.

With careful consideration, gaming consoles and devices have a lot of hidden potential for classroom application. Many students have these same game consoles at home, so they are used to using them already. Game quality is absolutely breathtaking because games produced for a console tend to have a much higher production budget than free browser-based games or game apps on mobile devices.

In their wonderfully original and insightful text, *Teach Math With the Wii: Engage Your K–7 Students Through Gaming Technology*, Meghan Hearn and Matthew Winner (2013) explore the amazing opportunities for learning-embedded mathematics within Nintendo Wii games. They provide readers with a list of potential games to use with students, lesson sparks for teachers to use with their students, and integration strategies to help teachers facilitate these new learning experiences in classrooms.

Many teachers might be left trying to imagine how to incorporate this into a classroom setting. *Wii Sports* is a console game for Nintendo Wii that consists of bowling, golf, baseball, tennis, and boxing. Many sports games are absolutely filled with embedded mathematics problems. Imagine these scenarios: a Nintendo Wii connected to an LCD projector and speakers, two controllers, and a *Wii Sports* game. As two students play golf, the teacher asks them to find the difference between their shots to see who drove the ball the furthest (subtraction), or each student can calculate how far she or he drove the golf ball during a set of shots (addition). In bowling, students can practice their basic mathematics by finding as many combinations as they can that add up to 10, or they can calculate how hight thier score was compared to others' by subtracting the final scores. In essence, game data are valuable sources of embedded mathematics. Most digital games (not just console games) teach our students without them realizing they are performing computations mentally. Game data can present themselves in the form of numbers, meters (fractions or percentages), graphs, rankings (ordinals), currency, and time. Teachers must simply imagine how to capture these embedded mathematics problems during the DGBL experience. The previously mentioned scenarios are just a snippet of the numerous opportunities console games offer students to learn in a fun and relevant way.

Due to the always-changing nature of gaming technologies, new systems replace older ones. Thanks to the launch of new gaming systems, old ones get a major price reduction. For example, a Nintendo Wii will run consumers about $70. Another idea is to ask students and parents to donate gently used consoles they are considering throwing out to classrooms adopting DGBL with console games.

There are also the portable game consoles such as Leapster for young learners and Nintendo DS. These portable consoles provide players with hands-on gameplay for a fraction of the cost of a larger console such as an Xbox. Also, they do not need a television or computer screen or speaker combination to provide the video and audio interface. At an average of one-third the cost of a traditional gaming system, portable consoles have serious potential for students, especially younger students. LeapFrog has a wide variety of educational games for young players such as *Letter Factory*, *Animal Genius*, or *Jake and the Never Land Pirates*.

App Markets: Tablets and Smartphones

With the astonishing evolution and popularity of smartphones and tablets, new digital distribution markets were created to provide mobile users with software applications, also known as *apps*, for easy purchase and download. The popularity of these new app markets led to the creation of a multibillion-dollar-a-year industry that didn't exist a few short years ago. The two major app markets are Apple's App Store, which serves users on Apple's operating system (iOS) devices such as the iPhone and iPad, and Google Play, which supplies apps to smartphones and tablets using the Android operating system platform. As of July 2014, Android users were able to choose between 1.3 million apps to download. Apple's App Store remained the second-largest app store with 1.2 million available apps. Windows, Amazon, and BlackBerry have their own smaller app markets with a combined seven hundred thousand available apps for download (Statisitca, 2014a, 2014b).

In each of the large app markets, the top two app categories for total downloads are *games* and *educational*. Members of the digital generation see mobile devices such as smartphones and tablets as tools for research, productivity, and digital storytelling, not just as sources for entertainment and distraction.

Many schools are adopting iPad or bring your own device (BYOD) initiatives to infuse more technology into classrooms in order to prepare their students for college and future careers. These readily available devices bring access to digital games directly to students. With their long battery life, wireless Internet access, and tactile interface, tablets have provided an intriguing technological solution for many school systems in the world.

Smartphones are another digital device that many middle and high school students have access to. With access to the same app markets as tablets, smartphones using Apple's iOS or Google's Android mobile operating system are another choice for gaming in the classroom. Teachers are able to take advantage of the powerful computers students carry in their pockets—the same devices they prefer to use.

The following are gaming apps that are absolute gems to incorporate into instruction.

The Oregon Trail: American Settler

The Oregon Trail: American Settler (www.gameloft.com/ipad -games/the-oregon-trail-american-settler-free) is a historical simulation game that allows players to build a town during the United States' westward expansion. Players must construct buildings, plant crops, raise livestock, generate revenue, and solve historically accurate problems of the era. This game explores key concepts in history, civics, economics, mathematics, and social studies.

Angry Birds

Angry Birds (www.rovio.com) is the megahit that launched (no pun intended) a feathery empire; players use birds as projectiles to defeat the evil pigs. The game has become so popular (over two billion downloads), Rovio has released several new games including *Angry Birds Space*, *Angry Birds: Rovio*, and *Angry Birds Star Wars* (Robertson, 2014). Despite its casual and silly nature, *Angry Birds* is filled with opportunities for classroom application. The game explores Newtonian physics, parabola, trajectory, cause and effect, trial and error, and strategy.

VocabularySpellingCity

VocabularySpellingCity (www.spellingcity.com/app) is an award-winning, game-based learning tool for vocabulary, spelling, writing, and language arts. The app (and service) offers dozens of learning games with the ability for teachers to track student performance.

DragonBox Algebra 5+

DragonBox Algebra 5+ (http://dragonboxapp.com) is a wonderful game (with great reviews) that gives players the opportunity to get a head start on learning algebra. Students as young as five can easily begin to grasp the basic processes involved in solving linear equations without even realizing they are learning.

Powers of Minus Ten

Powers of Minus Ten (http://powersofminusten.com) lets you zoom in to explore human cells and molecules! Discover some of the basic concepts in biology and learn about the structures of key cells, proteins, and molecules found in the human body. The iPad version includes instructional minigames.

ThinkerToy: Shapes

ThinkerToy: Shapes (http://thinkertoy.com) allows players to create objects with the use of tangrams. The app comes bundled with nearly one hundred picture puzzles to produce and is a fun way to explore geometry while being creative.

Math Duel: 2 Player Math Game

Math Duel: 2 Player Math Game (available on the App Store, Google Play, and Windows) allows two players to have fun at the same time! It is a fun educational game where two players compete against each other mathematically. This game helps students ages seven and up practice their basic mathematics facts (addition, subtraction, multiplication, and division) in a fun and engaging way.

Bridge Constructor

In *Bridge Constructor* (http://bridgeconstructor.com), players become a bridge engineer and architect in this building-simulation game. Players must create and design their own construction projects and watch the cars and trucks pass over them—or see them fall and crash while their inferior creations collapse due to weight and the laws of physics! The only limit for players in *Bridge Constructor* is the in-game budget constraints.

This list of gaming apps merely scratches the surface. With thousands of games spread across numerous platforms, the app markets are extraordinary resources to find potential games for tablets and smartphones. Each game available in app markets has a downloadable webpage with a game summary, content-rating system, and user reviews, making it possible to research a game to determine if it is a potential choice to use for learning. As always, educators must be aware that app markets are filled with entrepreneurs trying to sell products. These app designers are not experts in curriculum or instruction. Ultimately, teachers and curriculum developers must judge if a game or app is worthy to download and use with students. In chapter 2 (figure 2.1, page 26), readers will be privy to the criteria involved with selecting an ideal game for instruction.

The Most Popular Strategy for Finding Digital Games

It may not come as a shock, but teachers like to share what works in their classrooms. Many connected educators have flocked to social-media sites such as Twitter and Pinterest to share their aha moments, classroom solutions (often referred to as *hacks*), and lesson ideas. Inversely, many educators comb these social-media sites to find, learn about, and implement classroom or instructional solutions. In *Level Up Learning*, almost seven hundred teachers share their experiences using gaming in their classrooms (Takeuchi & Vaala, 2014). The survey suggests most teachers share information about potential instructional games to use with students through informal channels such as teacher-to-teacher interactions.

Although the word-of-mouth method is great to generate interest and help educators find potential games to use for DGBL, many teachers new to this teaching approach would benefit from an engaging, gaming-rich workshop or professional development program where they can explore gameplay, discuss pedagogical strategies, generate and share resources, and make connections in their local school districts for support and collaboration.

> Game-based learning is getting very popular, but finding support remains difficult. Still, most education conferences are adding games and learning tracks, or at least adding games to their ed-tech tracks. In addition, most game developers recognize that professional development is one of the biggest obstacles to adoption, so they often provide video tutorials and other materials for teachers on their websites. (Shapiro, Salen, Schwartz, & Darvasi, 2014, p. 17)

If attending a workshop such as this in person is difficult, then a virtual conference is a possibility. Workshops, conferences, and extended professional development programs will allow for educators to develop a deeper understanding of the benefits, challenges, and effective teaching and assessment strategies essential to implementing and facilitating a DGBL experience in a learning environment.

Perhaps a more pragmatic approach is necessary to find good-quality digital learning games and propagate effective learning strategies to use with them—create a gaming-centered professional learning network (PLN), or what educators with an interest in teaching with games refer to as a guild. Several examples of these guilds include World of Warcraft (WoW) in School, Gamers Advancing Meaningful Education (G.A.M.E.), and Education Gaming Guild (EGG).

Experienced DGBL facilitators must share their knowledge with others, both locally and globally. They can easily lead a group of interested educators in work groups, instructional gaming book chats, or workshops. This grassroots approach is the most effective and realistic method of indoctrinating more DGBL facilitators.

Chapter 2
Evaluating and Field Testing Digital Games

Not all digital games are created equal. Although the gaming market is saturated with potential games, many fall short in quality or academic rigor. According to writer Jordan Shapiro, "The best learning games teach in the same way good teachers teach: They don't trick students into being interested, they help students find genuine excitement in learning a subject" (quoted in Shapiro et al., 2014, p. 20). Educators must always begin with their curriculum source. For many educators, this involves consulting their school-based, district, or state curriculum, or perhaps educators must consult the Common Core State Standards for English language arts and mathematics (National Governors Association Center for Best Practices & Council of Chief State School Officers, 2010a, 2010b).

Traditional forms of lesson planning require educators to start with the learning objective. Then they find the tools and resources essential to help students achieve these learning objectives, and finally, they consider what instructional and assessment strategies to employ to reach all learners. This formula can still work with a DGBL experience, but it will probably be easier to start with a potential game, then structure learning experiences around the game. *Planning outward* such as this may seem nonsensical to educators, but the simple fact is that a lot of digital games were not constructed with the purpose of being used in a classroom during a lesson. Either way, DGBL facilitators must consider what they are teaching to students and find a game that aligns with the desired student learning outcomes. As you play or pilot available digital games, reflect on the following questions (figure 2.1) to determine if the game is ideal for integration.

Learning Outcomes and Pedagogy

- ☐ Does gameplay support the learning objectives or expected student outcome(s)?

- ☐ Can you use multiple games during instruction to address more or all of the learning objectives or expected student outcome(s)?

- ☐ Is gameplay realistic, and does it involve skills that are useful in the real world?

- ☐ Will the game challenges evolve with better player performance?

- ☐ Is the game fun, engaging, and challenging for players?

- ☐ Is one game better aligned with the expected learning outcomes than the others?

- ☐ Will gameplay address other content areas to provide a multidisciplinary experience for the students?

- ☐ Is the game a teaching game or a testing game? How do you intend to use it with your students?

Assessment

- ☐ Does the game contain assessment tools or performance measurements to provide users and instructors with player feedback?

☐ Can the game-based facilitator (educator) incorporate reality-based assessment strategies; measuring knowledge attained during gameplay?

☐ How might the game be incorporated into classroom instruction or assessment?

Technical Aspects

☐ Is the audio-visual presentation of the game clearly visible and audible, and does it provide an appealing aesthetic experience?

☐ Are there enough game stations to promote a low enough student-to-game ratio?

☐ Are appropriate peripherals and accessibility tools provided to each game station for the gaming experience?

☐ Is the game control or manipulation transparent, intuitive, and logical for players?

☐ Is the digital-game content appropriate for the students' academic or maturity level?

Figure 2.1: Checklist to plan and prepare for a DGBL experience.

*Visit **go.solution-tree.com/technology** for a reproducible version of this figure.*

The second consideration for evaluating a digital game to incorporate into instruction is to identify what type of game is being used. Karl Kapp, an instructional technology professor at Bloomsburg University and a pioneer in the field of using digital games and gamification to teach, states that there are two types of games. The first type is testing games.

> Testing Games are games where the learner already needs to know the information to be successful. The focus of the game is not to apply knowledge but rather to recall knowledge . . . If you want to test knowledge,

testing games are fine but do not expect learning to occur. (Kapp, 2013)

The second type is teaching games: "Teaching games, on the other hand, do not test knowledge; they impart knowledge. This is accomplished through a series of activities within the game that teaches the learner what he or she needs to do" (Kapp, 2013).

As digital games continue to evolve, these two classifications of testing and teaching games begin to blur, because more and more games are becoming both—first they teach the gamer, then they test or assess the gamer's understanding of the content or skill the gamer learns or develops.

Kapp's game classifications become valuable for facilitators considering a digital game for the learning process. Facilitators must select a teaching game to teach their students and a testing game to assess or reinforce previously learned information. An ideal teaching game is *iCivics: Branches of Power*, a simulation-based game that teaches players about the three branches of the U.S. government during gameplay. A good testing game is *Jeopardy!*, a game that only assesses previously acquired knowledge. As facilitators search for games to use in the classroom, it is important for them to consider how the game will be used. If students need to learn new information, then facilitators must locate a teaching game. A testing game would be ideal for assessment or a review of learned concepts. Differentiating the two game types is fairly straightforward. If content is introduced to the player, then the game is most likely teaching. If the game starts to ask questions and expects the answers from the very beginning, then the game fits neatly into the testing category. With advances in gaming technologies and storytelling, more and more games are starting to be classified as both teaching and testing games.

The perfect example of a teaching and testing digital game is Teachley's *Addimal Adventure*. In the game, players are instructed in the many strategies for mathematics computation in a visually appealing virtual learning environment with constant feedback and reward. The app, available through Apple's App Store, also uses data analytics to measure and track student performance, as well as what Common Core standards and other benchmarks players have met.

When facilitators have narrowed their search results to a few or one potential game, they must play it. This gameplay can't be superficial—it must be experienced, evaluated, and critiqued for efficacy. A pragmatic approach for evaluating a potential digital game is to ask colleagues to help during the evaluation process. A small group of educators (or even students) can pilot gameplay and uncover what the game's strengths and weaknesses are. Once this vetting process is complete and a game has been selected for a DGBL activity, facilitators must determine what learning and assessment strategies to implement for fun and engagement with their students.

Learning With Digital Games: Strategies That Work

Using games (digital and nondigital) with students during the learning and assessment process does not isolate educators; it empowers them and allows for a transformation in the role they assume in the classroom. Digital game-based facilitators are able to adopt additional duties during the learning process.

> Using games in a meaningful way within lessons depended far more on the effective use of existing teaching skills than it did on the development of any new, game-related skills. Far from being sidelined, teachers were required to take a central role in scaffolding and supporting students' learning through games. (Sandford, Ulicsak, Facer, & Rudd, 2006, p. 4)

As students learn from and experience gameplay, facilitators have the ability to circulate around the learning environment and help students who need it, conduct discussions and ask questions with learners to gauge their understanding, or adjust gaming tasks for those pupils who need more challenges. With the assistance of digital games, facilitators have the potential to transform learning by taking the dependence and attention off teachers during lessons and placing it on the game and students where it belongs.

Many of the traditional elements of a lesson plan can be infused with digital gaming. A similar form of media having such a profoundly positive and popular impact on learning is the use of video or movies. Everything from full-feature movies, to YouTube clips, to short Vine and Instagram footage has been used to relay information to students. Learners have also used video to create authentic instructional artifacts to demonstrate competencies in written and spoken language, storytelling, and their understanding of acquired knowledge. Many of the same opportunities educators have used to infuse multimedia elements such as video into a lesson are transferrable to using digital games. The following are some easy-to-implement instructional strategies facilitators can use to promote fun and engaging learning experiences using digital games during a lesson. In addition to each strategy being defined, a game is selected and a scenario is included to envision the strategy in action.

Lesson Motivation

In many traditional lesson-planning formats, a short motivation or warm-up is used to prime and engage learners for new information. Facilitators can have students play a digital game to start a lesson. The allotted time should be relatively short—perhaps five to ten minutes. During this time, facilitators help gamers uncover the purpose for gameplay by asking questions to activate prior knowledge and connecting the embedded concepts to the expected learning outcomes for the lesson. Afterward, facilitators debrief with players to reflect on gameplay and connect it with new concepts or skills being explored in the next learning event of the lesson.

An example of this strategy would be if students were learning about recycling, reusing, and reducing in the environment. *Sort Your Waste* (www.kidsgoflash.com/games/sort_your_waste.html) is a web browser–based game kidsGoflash produces where players make good environmental decisions through recycling or trashing certain household items. Before gameplay, the facilitator introduces the game to players, asks them to predict what the game will be about, plays the game for a few moments while students watch to introduce game controls and navigation, and then allows them to play. Facilitators ask questions that draw out and examine key concepts explored during gameplay at the end of the allotted game time. For *Sort Your Waste*, these questions include:

- What were you able to recycle in the game?

- What did you have to throw into the trash can?

- Were there any items you discovered that could be recycled?

- What are some things you know you can recycle that weren't in the game?

Free Play

Free play allows gamers to explore digital games without much interference from their teachers. Ultimately, students are given free rein to explore, fail, retry, reflect, and learn from the game in an unstructured environment. The facilitator circulates around the learning environment and carefully observes each gamer as the students play to learn. During their observations, facilitators must record what they witness during their students' gameplay and assist any learners who are struggling or adjust the learning scenario if the learners are not being challenged enough.

The facilitator must select an effective follow-up activity for learners to demonstrate their mastery of the content. These activities could include classroom discussion, creative writing, journaling, blogging, creating a multimedia product, or participating in a simulation or role play.

In PBS KIDS's *Mad Money* (http://pbskids.org/itsmylife/games/mad_money_flash.html), gamers must save money over the course of thirty mock days to purchase a big-ticket item of their selection. In the game, players visit shops, perform chores, collect bonuses, and receive penalties on their way to their financial goal. *Mad Money* is fairly user friendly, so players should pick up how to play it rather easily. After gameplay, students can research and create their own monthly budget to either save money or buy a big-ticket item of their choosing. This example is but one potential gaming scenario that sprouts from free gameplay.

Baseline to Finish Line

This strategy involves having students play the selected game twice—once before formal class instruction on the targeted learning involved in the game and the second after the learning has occurred. During the first gaming session, referred to as the baseline, facilitators circulate around to students playing the selected digital game and record student performance (if the game doesn't already do so). A student's performance becomes a baseline score—a raw measure of the student's current understanding of the targeted concepts explored in the game before being formally taught during a lesson. After instruction occurs, students play the same digital game again while the facilitator observes their performance during a second gameplay session known as the finish line.

Digital game–based facilitators should see improved performance during gameplay the second time around as they conduct in-process evaluations of student learning needs and academic progress during instruction otherwise known as formative assessment.

To envision this strategy in action, Funbrain hosts a testing game called the *Periodic Table Game* (www.funbrain.com/funbrain /periodic). The game asks players to name certain elements when given symbols and tracks correct and incorrect answers. The facilitator asks players to play two rounds and records their score out of a possible score of twenty. This initial score becomes their baseline scores. After students experience their formal learning lessons involving the periodic table, they play the game again in the hopes of scoring higher than their baseline scores. Both facilitators and students can see academic growth over time. If a student scores lower or relatively the same on his or her finish line score as he or she did on the baseline, then that student might need reteaching or an alternative approach to learning about the periodic table.

Setting a Mental Stage

Digital games help create context. At times, educators have difficulty establishing the importance of what students are learning in class. It is particularly challenging for teachers to demonstrate the real-world relevance of everything students learn when they are forced to do so in the same location, with the same surroundings every day. Digital games and interactive simulations have the ability to immerse students into new and exciting learning experiences and establish that crucial need for instructional relevance.

A great example of the immersive nature of digital games and simulations is *Lifeboat to Mars* (http://pbskids.org/lifeboat), an ecosystem-simulation game PBS KIDS Go! hosts. Students learn the basics of ecosystems as they participate in the game's tutorials, missions, and microworld levels. Students experience science concepts and read challenging and engaging text with the main purpose of creating an ecosystem capable of supporting terrestrial life on Mars. Although they remain in their classrooms on planet Earth, mentally they are on Mars attempting to bring life to the red planet. *Lifeboat to Mars* helps students explore important scientific concepts while creating a fun and engaging context to learn in.

Gaming With Anticipation

Facilitators select a game students will play during class. However, before gameplay begins, students are given several questions they must answer during or after gameplay. Similar to an anticipation guide, which is a reading-comprehension strategy that is used before reading to activate students' prior knowledge and build curiosity about a new topic, players are asked several questions to help develop their interest in the game and its embedded instructional topics and concepts. Questions can be formatted in multiple choice, true or false, or fill in the blank—any format conducive for quick, short-form responses.

Mission US: Mission 3—A Cheyenne Odyssey (www.mission-us.org /pages/mission-3) is an educational role-playing game in which gamers take on the role of Little Fox—a young Cheyenne boy in the 19th century. Assuming the role of Little Fox, players are immersed into a historical simulation rich in logical reasoning, investigation, and multiculturalism. Before gamers take on the challenge, facilitators have them answer the following anticipatory-guide questions.

1. Are the Cheyenne children similar to you: *Yes* or *No*

2. Little Fox belongs to the Northern Cheyenne tribe: *True* or *False*

3. Select the setting the Cheyenne tribe called home: *Mountains*, *Plains*, or *Desert*

Once the students have played the game, have them revisit the questions to answer them. These short-form questions can lead the facilitator and his or her students into a deeper discussion about the game and its content.

Teams and Tournaments

Games are a natural mental construct for students to develop the fundamentals of teamwork and provide situational learning where they cultivate their collaborative skills. Through team-based games, players begin to understand the basic advantages of cooperative learning, such as the division of labor, benefit of pooling group knowledge to develop collective intelligence, and increased productivity. Working in collaborative learning groups also develops important interpersonal skills and morals—players explore the concepts of fairness, group dynamics, leadership, and responsibility.

Implementing teams during gameplay also has the benefit of using fewer technological resources since players are typically taking turns. Gamers must share a common goal. They must also win or fail as a team. A classic example of a game that can utilize teamwork is *Jeopardy!*. JeopardyLabs (https://jeopardylabs .com) allows facilitators to create *Jeopardy!* games online for free. JeopardyLabs can provide games for any grade level and academic content area. A facilitator can divide his or her class into two teams, and each team takes turns answering review questions. Team members for each team select questions, discuss answers, and celebrate or lament *together*.

Tournaments are another team-based game format that increases the competition drastically. Typically groups are much smaller and function in a manner where they either succeed or fail. In the multiplication game *Grand Prix Multiplication* (www.arcademics.com /games/grand_prix/grand_prix.html), the facilitator has student team members take turns performing the race. The goal of the game is to receive the fastest time around a racetrack as players answer multiplication problems. Each member of the team participates in the race, and all members add their results together for a combined score. The fastest team either wins or moves on to the next stage of the tournament.

When using teams or a tournament structure in an educational gaming environment, facilitators must look for ways for students to productively interact, equitably divide work, and share responsibility and accountability for success and failure. Facilitators have free rein to design and implement activities outside of the digital game to enhance the collaborative or competitive nature of gameplay. They can ask students questions, track and reward team progress, or provide gamers with an opportunity to reflect on gameplay or apply their knowledge to a follow-up task, activity, or challenge.

A Learning Event

In essence, the daily instructional lessons educators teach are a series of instructional events woven into a tapestry for learners. As schools embrace new learning tools and resources, the instructional resources at the fingertips of educators and students alike evolve. In the 1980s and 1990s, using video to teach was not as widespread in schools as it is today. At the start of the new millennium, schools struggled to supply every classroom with an instructionally valid computer station connected to the Internet. Likewise, many school systems are struggling to fund other instructional tools such as interactive whiteboards, document cameras, or laptops and tablets. Despite the struggle, new tools are entering classrooms daily, causing the media and tools they use to learn to expand greatly.

Most digital games easily available to students are short-form games or games that tend to take very little time to play or have premises that are easy to follow and master.

> Played in small doses, short-form games can serve as great interactive examples, reinforcing and supplementing a teacher-driven curriculum. Short-form games tend to work best for learning when they're focused on a specific skill set or concept. Think of them like brief simulations. (Shapiro et al., 2014, p. 22)

A short-form game can easily be implemented as a learning event inside a lesson plan. The key for success is preparing students to play the game and debriefing with them afterward. Preparation can be achieved when facilitators ask guiding questions, conduct classroom discussions, or provide a game preview for learners. Debriefing after gameplay can involve a facilitator asking questions or holding discussions with students or having them use their newly acquired or refined knowledge to create an educational artifact.

Learning events embedded in lessons vary in regards to the time needed to implement them, the resources they require, and the instructional strategies needed to make the content stick for students. A digital game can be implemented to fit many different learning situations, within different instructional time frames, using numerous instructional approaches.

The "Long Experience" of Playing and Learning

The previous section made the case for using short-form games during instruction. Whether used during a warm-up, a review, or a lesson event, or as a catalyst for cooperative learning, DGBL fits into many lesson plans *if* the game is short enough to complete before moving on to the next part of the lesson. Yet what about the games that do not fit neatly into a ten-minute warm-up, a thirty-minute review, or even a sixty-minute lesson plan? What about long-form games?

Long-form games have extensive story lines or virtual environments that take gamers more time to complete than short-form games. Julius Caesar said it best, "Experience is the teacher of all things" (Blanchard, 2010). The following game types provide a wealth of experiences for players to learn from—providing an incredible opportunity for experiential learning, or learning by doing.

Minecraft and *MinecraftEdu*

Minecraft (https://minecraft.net) is a popular game that has been taking the gaming world by storm. Developed by Swedish game developer Mojang, *Minecraft* is an open-world building game where players use blocks to build in creative mode. The game has become such a popular hit that many educators have taken advantage of its popularity and functionality to teach the digital generation.

Playing *Minecraft*, like many long-form games, takes an extensive amount of time to complete. However, the potential for experiential and multidisciplinary learning more than makes up for the instructional time used during learning.

MinecraftEdu (http://minecraftedu.com) observes the hidden potential of *Minecraft* in learning and offers educational solutions, support, and ideas to its customers to help them integrate the game into schools. Educators use *MinecraftEdu* to explore hundreds of concepts in multiple disciplines. In "Math," players can explore concepts such as addition, subtraction, multiplication, and volume. In "History," students can construct historical structures such as the pyramids of Giza or the Roman Coliseum. In "Science," gamers can explore concepts such as landforms, the life cycle, and biomes. There are also options for social studies, art, language arts—the list of potential learning experiences educators can facilitate with their students goes on and on.

The Sandbox and *The Sandbox EDU*

Minecraft is not the only game on the market with this powerful potential in experiential learning. Pixowl's *The Sandbox* (www.thesandboxgame.com) shares many of the same game characteristics as *Minecraft*. The player crafts his or her own universe through the exploration of resources (such as water, soil, lightning, lava, sand, and glass) and many more complex elements (such as humans, zombies, robots, dinosaurs, monuments, wildlife, animals, trees, gems, vehicles, sensors, explosives, and wondrous contraptions). *The Sandbox* also has an educational version known as *The Sandbox EDU* (www.thesandboxgame.com/education) that includes lesson ideas and resources for teachers ready to embrace gaming on their Apple devices.

WoW in School

Many other long-form digital games exist for rich learning experiences in many academic subjects. Peggy Sheehy and Lucas Gillispie, two amazing educators, developed WoW in School (http://wowinschool.pbworks.com/w/page/5268731/FrontPage) —a language arts curriculum developed around the extremely popular and incredibly immersive, massively multiplayer online role-play game known as *World of Warcraft*. The narrative-rich story lines of the game provide students with exciting opportunities to develop their reading and writing skills.

Lure of the Labyrinth

Hosted by Thinkport (a product of a partnership between Maryland Public Television and the Johns Hopkins University Center for Technology in Education), *Lure of the Labyrinth* (https://labyrinth .thinkport.org/www) is a long-form digital game for middle school students learning pre-algebra. It includes a wealth of intriguing mathematics-based puzzles wrapped into an exciting narrative game where the players' ultimate goal is to find their lost pet while saving the world from monsters. The game is linked to the Common Core State Standards and gives students a chance to actually think like mathematicians.

There is an abundant supply of long-form games for facilitators to choose from. Although using these types of games requires an extensive amount of time for students to play and learn, the investment is well spent considering students are engaged in numerous learning experiences wrapped in an immersive story line with better production quality than the quick-to-produce, short-form games you can find rather easily online.

Chapter 3
Gaming and Instructional Assessment

Instructional assessment has long been considered unpleasant for educators and students alike. The overuse of quizzes and high-stakes testing has created an atmosphere of tension, uncertainty, and stress in the education system. In fact, due to the practice of excessive testing, many schools sacrifice curriculum and rigor to prepare students to test well. For the learner, the process of assessment is like taking cough syrup—a distasteful elixir that will make them sleepy or foggy. Many traditional forms of assessment judge, classify, or even pigeonhole students, leaving them disoriented and foggy about what the assessment really accomplishes. Oftentimes, too much weight is allotted to traditional forms of assessment such as standardized tests to determine if a student will receive placement in honor classes, entry into top-tier universities, and eventually a fast track to a high-salary career.

For educators, assessments have become the driving force for everything! High-stakes testing determines what students learn, how they learn, where they learn, what facilities they use, what programs will be funded, what equipment they use, and how their performance will be evaluated. This educational formula stifles educators and students alike. A great deal of instructional time is rationed off for test preparation and implementation. The final straw is tying teacher evaluation to test performance. There are far too many factors that go into teacher evaluation—test results must not be the most important or only reason an educator keeps her or his job.

Summative Assessment

Truthfully, the education system relies too heavily on summative assessments like standardized tests, unit tests, and quizzes. By definition, summative assessments are used to evaluate student learning at the end of an instructional unit or time period by comparing them against some standard or benchmark. Summative assessments can be useful to determine strengths and weaknesses in curriculum design and instructional delivery. They also provide a very detailed snapshot of the learner if they are well aligned to instruction.

However, this type of assessment only provides a brief glimpse of the learner. Educators, administrators, parents, and politicians should not simply settle for one snapshot to determine a student's academic success. All of these educational stakeholders should demand to see the entire photo album of snapshots! Summative assessment results should be one performance data point out of many data points.

Imagine a young learner; let's call her Hope. She is a bright, articulate young student who is energetic, sociable, creative, and very hardworking. She takes a timed bubble test filled with low-order thinking questions asking her to recall what she has memorized or read in a dense block of random text. She fails miserably. Hope is not dumb! Hope is not lazy! Hope is not a student with a learning disability or a developmental issue, or a slow learner. Hope is a student learning in an education system that depends too heavily on summative assessments to weigh student, school, district, and national success.

Summative assessments have their place in education but not as the driving force for educational reform, funding, and determining if a teacher is effective or not. Assessment must be a process where teachers and students come together and determine where they are now and where they want to go in the future, and uncover or plot the path to get there. Assessment does not have to anesthetize Hope. It should invigorate her and her teachers to set a course for academic and personal success.

DGBL has entered assessment practices with the hopes of measuring not only content-specific knowledge, but soft skills such as problem solving, creativity, and collaboration at the same time, through the mechanics and narrative of the game. There is a strong possibility that one day, in the not-so-distant future, students will take a standardized test by playing a digital game. In fact, many educational research institutions and think tanks are already working on creating powerful learning and assessment experiences for the digital generation. GlassLab, a collaborative team-up of the Institute of Play, the Entertainment Software Association, Electronic Arts, Educational Testing Service, and Pearson's Center for Digital Data, Analytics & Adaptive Learning, "is exploring the potential for existing, commercially successful digital games to serve both as potent learning environments and real-time assessments of student learning" (Institute of Play, 2014).

However, it is currently ill advised for educators to use digital games they find in a catalog or through a web search as summative assessments. Instruction and assessment must be aligned, or it could spell disaster for the learner. For instance, if a student plays a bunch of digital mathematics games as instruction and then takes a paper-and-pencil quiz based on the concepts explored during gameplay, then the student is participating in an assessment that is misaligned. How does the facilitator know that the student will be able to transfer her or his game-based learning experiences to the traditional quiz? The facilitator is changing too many variables for the assessment results to be valid and reliable. Instructional methods must be aligned to assessment methods.

Repetition: Test-Taking Preparation and Review

Facilitators don't have to wait for game designers to get the learning and assessment formula correct in digital games. Digital games are valuable tools when used to review and prepare for summative assessments. Cognitive scientists find great promise in spaced repetition—the process of learners studying information in blocks over longer periods of time. Instead of cramming study sessions into a short time period, the learner would learn and relearn content over a longer time period: "The spacing effect is one of the oldest and best documented phenomena in the history of learning and memory research" (Bahrick & Hall, 2005, as quoted in Thalheimer, 2006, p. 3).

By framing review sessions in a game over an extended time period using spaced repetition, learners are able to help content stick for both unit and standardized tests with the added benefits of engagement, fun, and excitement. There are numerous tools that educators can use to create these review games. The tool should be easy to use, versatile, and adaptable to numerous classroom environments. Socrative (www.socrative.com) lets teachers engage and assess their students with instructional activities on most digital devices. Through the use of real-time questioning, instant result aggregation, and visualization, teachers can determine their classes' understanding. QuizBreak! (http://clear.msu.edu/quizbreak), Zondle (www.zondle.com/publicPagesv2), and Review Game Zone (http://reviewgamezone.com) are additional tools available at no cost for educators to construct their own review games.

Formative Assessment

Unlike summative assessment, which is completed at the end of the instructional process, formative assessment is ongoing and used by both teachers and students to evaluate and make adjustments during their learning experiences. It's a critical way for teachers to check students' understanding and then use the information to guide instruction.

Formative assessment helps create and renew the learning process. Its goal is to monitor student learning and provide ongoing feedback that educators should use to improve their teaching and students should use to improve their learning. Unlike the linear design of summative assessment, formative assessment is more like a perpetual cycle where educators continuously guide students to access their prior knowledge, engage them in learning activities to build on their knowledge base, demonstrate their instructional gains (through numerous assessment methods), and reflect on the learning. After this cycle is completed, the entire process begins anew.

A-GAMES (Analyzing Games for Assessment in Math, ELA/ Social Studies, and Science) is a collaboration between New York University and the University of Michigan. A study, *Empowering Educators: Supporting Student Progress in the Classroom With Digital Games* (Fishman, Riconscente, Snider, Tsai, & Plass, 2014), finds that educators who use digital games for the formative assessment of facts and knowledge, concepts, and big ideas and the mastery of specific skills are more likely to use these assessments to track student progress, give feedback to students, and check for student engagement and motivation on a daily basis. The study also shows that the teachers who use digital games during instruction are more likely to use formative-assessment techniques in their classrooms. What are these specific formative-assessment practices? The answers include many of the techniques teachers use every day such as observing students, having classroom discussion, reviewing student work, using every pupil response (EPR), asking probing and guiding questions, and peeking over students' shoulders during work time.

Stealth Assessment

According to Valerie Shute and Matthew Ventura (2013),

> Stealth assessment is woven directly and invisibly into the fabric of the learning or gaming environment. During game play, students naturally produce rich sequences of actions while performing complex tasks, drawing on the very skills or competencies that we want to assess.

Instead of the assessment being isolated from the learning process, it is embedded in it, so players are constantly learning and being evaluated. Hidden assessment such as this will also prevent students from changing their behavior due to anxiety, which in turn will produce more accurate data on student performance. Since the assessment is also situational (embedded in gameplay), the gamer is "focused on the situation, which provides a better approximation of how he or she would behave in a similar real-world situation" (Derosier, 2014).

For educators, using stealth assessment might seem like a far-fetched dream. However, digital games are systems that can capture just as much data as they transmit to the gamer. Player performance can be collected by technology systems or educators using traditional means such as classroom observation to assess student performance or make informed instructional decisions. Stealth assessment is an intriguing benefit of digital gaming, and as learning games evolve, the assessment tools will become more robust and transparent for educators to use with their students for deep, powerful learning.

Learning Analytics

Educators are such hard workers. They plan engaging lessons every day, grade papers, and champion their students' academic growth. However, no matter how well trained and observant teachers are, they can't capture every single achievement, success, obstacle, mistake, or challenge each of their fifteen, twenty, thirty, or even one hundred students experience every day. After all, teachers are only human (OK—incredible, hardworking, and dedicated humans).

Technology systems such as computers, gaming consoles, and mobile devices easily collect user data. Every choice, every decision, every answer, and every experience the player makes is logged and stored automatically. This unbelievable access to raw data has created a powerful mathematical science known as data analytics. Many companies and organizations use data analytics to make better business decisions, and the sciences use digital analytics to verify or disprove existing models, theories, and beliefs. Education's variant of this science is known as learning analytics. Instead of technology systems logging consumer behavior and purchase habits, which are commonly the case in digital analytics, learning analytics focus on student data such as online behavior, assessment results, and learning preferences. With more and more data being collected about learners, the analysis should help provide the educational field with statistically supported evidence of what works and doesn't work in the classroom.

If designed to, digital games can capture so many data points about players that they become like a second set of eyes for teachers. They can collect how many correct and incorrect answers a player provides; they can track user progress through a story line or narrative; they can even capture instances of gameplay. The games are doing this while providing immediate feedback and reward to the player. Educators can use these data to improve instruction and target students who need extra assistance.

Teachley games and apps provide the perfect example of learning analytics at work in digital games.

> Teachley is an educational technology company whose mission is to improve and help shape the future of teaching and learning. Founded by former teachers and experts in children's cognition and learning, Teachley uses cognitive science research to create educational apps that teach effective learning strategies and assess what kids know within engaging games. (Carpenter, Pager, & Labrecque, 2013)

To date, Teachley has produced *Addimal Adventure* and *Mt. Multiplis*, two teaching games that introduce players to memorization and problem-solving strategies to learn operational fluency in early mathematics education. These two games, available in Apple's App Store, are impressive enough, but the background data collection and analytics are truly revolutionary. Teachley Analytics collects students' user data as they play and generates reports for educators to analyze. These reports help educators determine in a heartbeat the students who are excelling in their computational practices and the students who need remediation. The games also provide players with considerable feedback and reports to assist them in setting future learning goals.

Teachley is not the only game developer bringing web-tracking practices into the classroom. VocabularySpellingCity provides spelling, vocabulary, writing, and language arts activities for K–12 crosscurricular word study. Educators using VocabularySpellingCity are able to automate the administration and grading of spelling and vocabulary tests. It also provides educators with progress monitoring and the option to differentiate learning experiences for students when necessary. For science education, Science4Us provides young science students with interactivities, simulations, and games for students to learn from.

Teacher support and training are also huge services for all of these learning game suites. Each offers just-in-time training (learning conducted when it has become necessary and needed by the learner), support, and lesson ideas, so educators do not have to reinvent the wheel when it comes to planning learning experiences for their students.

Digital games could have a potentially large role in the learning analytics field. Due in part to digital games being provided to players through technology systems such as computers and mobile devices, every learning experience can be logged and added to the large pools of data currently being collected in local school, state, or provincial systems nationally and even one day globally to improve the ways educators teach their students.

Takeaways for Readers

DGBL is beginning to pick up steam in popularity and is generating serious buzz in the education realm. Despite its interest, educators are left in search of support and ideas for implementing learning games in the classroom. In this section of the book, you are provided with some parting gifts that will be extremely valuable for facilitators implementing DGBL experiences with their students.

Takeaway 1: Five Educational Super Blogs for Digital Learning

The following are five of some of the very best education blogs involving digital learning. Oftentimes, these blogs publish very insightful articles about gaming in education.

Edutopia

Produced by the George Lucas Educational Foundation, *Edutopia* (www.edutopia.org) documents and disseminates cutting-edge classroom practices about project-based learning, student teams working cooperatively, students connecting with passionate experts, and broader forms of assessment. It also focuses on new digital multimedia and telecommunications that can support these practices and engage students.

MindShift

MindShift (http://blogs.kqed.org/mindshift) was created by KQED and NPR to explore the many dimensions of learning, including cultural and technology trends, innovations in education, research, education policy, and more.

TeachThought

TeachThought (www.teachthought.com) supports K–12 educators in evolving learning for 21st century students. Its primary interest is exploring emerging learning models, such as blended learning, project-based learning, and self-directed learning, while simultaneously exploring the role of play in learning and supporting educators' professional development.

Edudemic

The goal of *Edudemic* (www.edudemic.com) is to connect teachers, administrators, students, and just about everyone else with the best technology on the planet. It has grown to become one of the leading education technology sites on the web. It's become a vibrant forum of discussion, discovery, and knowledge. The site features a regular flow of tools, tips, resources, visuals, and guest posts from dozens of authors around the world.

InfoSavvy21

Originally conceived by Ian Jukes decades ago under the title of the *Committed Sardines* blog, *InfoSavvy21* (www.infosavvy21 .com/blog) now hosts a blog that examines everything associated with teaching the digital generation using cutting-edge best practices. This blog features a regular stream of teaching strategies, tools, resources, and posts from numerous authors around the world.

Takeaway 2: *Evernote* Public Notebook

Using a wonderful (and free) app known as *Evernote*, I have spent over five years collecting and curating web content, journal articles, and research studies associated with digital gaming and learning. Visit http://bit.ly/GamesLearningAssessmentTools to access a dynamic database of digital-gaming materials and resources. With over one hundred pages of content (and additional pages added daily), this *Evernote* notebook is like purchasing a supplemental text.

Takeaway 3: Digital Learning Game Database

In a joint effort between seasoned educator Devin DeLange and me, the Digital Learning Game Database (DLGD) was conceptualized to archive and curate digital games with learning potential. One of the biggest barriers of incorporating digital games into lessons is the struggle involved with finding good games for deep, immersive learning. The database's entries are categorized by subject area, with short summaries of the game along with concept and skills tags to identify what the game helps to teach or test. The games are also categorized by gaming platform such as web based, desktop, console, or mobile markets (such as Apple iOS and Google Play). The Digital Learning Game Database (http://bit.ly/DigitalLearningGameDatabase) has over one hundred games for visitors to search through and is perpetually growing with new games added daily to help facilitators deliver quality DGBL experiences to learners.

Takeaway 4: DLGD Participation

Crowdsourcing is such a powerful phenomenon in the age of the Internet. It allows people to band together and perform incredible feats of productivity and altruism. The perfect example of the power of crowdsourcing and social media is the ALS (amyotrophic lateral sclerosis) Association Ice Bucket Challenge. During the challenge, participants engaged in a simple, temporarily unpleasant stunt (pouring cold water on themselves) and shared it on social-networking sites such as Facebook and Twitter to spread awareness of ALS and solicit donations to fund research and clinical-management projects to combat the disease.

The ALS Ice Bucket Challenge took advantage of the participatory nature of digital culture. It was a litmus test to prove the existence of a powerful social fabric that our need to connect to one another perpetuates. We can use this power to crowdsource a new tool to help educators find the digital games they need for powerful and immersive learning with digital learners. If readers find a digital game educators could use with students, then they can visit the online form (http://bit.ly/DLGDEntryForm) to add it to the extensive list.

Leveling Up Classrooms

Using digital games during the learning and assessment process can add a great deal of motivation, engagement, and fun for learners. As time moves on, the sheer number of produced games will continue to grow, the quality of games will improve even more than the cinematic-quality titles hitting the market every day, and more and more people will adopt gaming as a hobby. As for education, digital games will continue to creep into classroom after classroom as educators leverage their immersive and engaging manner with the always-on generation.

As a cautionary note, digital games should never be overutilized in schools because they will lose their appeal for both students and teachers. Instead, educational gaming should become another approach for educators to consider adding to their toolbox of teaching strategies—pulled out when the time and learning situation call for it.

If readers recall, I mentioned an unsolved equation at the beginning of the book: Hard Work + Deep Fun = ?. As the author, it is not up to me to answer this equation. It is up to the hard-working and dedicated educators helping prepare students for the future to fill in the blank. Today's educators must find a common ground to reach the students of the digital age. This can be done by embracing the digital generation's tools and ways. With the stress of high-stakes testing, increased teacher accountability, and new initiatives such as the Common Core, it is safe to say that educators have a lot on their plates. However, embracing new teaching approaches—especially ones that are fun and intellectually appetizing to students—is a no-brainer.

Appendix: Discussion Questions

This text was written with the exclusive purpose of providing educators with new ideas to use with their students. Professional development can be challenging for teachers. The following are discussion questions related to the content of the book. Readers have their choice on how to use these questions. First, the list can act as personal reflection questions for readers to contemplate after they have read the book. Next, readers can elicit others to conduct a book club and conduct their own form of professional development with their colleagues. Finally, the questions can be used for professional research to fuel self-inquiry and curiosity. Whatever the case, the discussion questions are provided to extend readers' experience.

1. What are the main differences in how students learn nowadays versus how students learned in the past?

2. What are the factors making digital game–based learning (DGBL) possible for adoption now or in the near future?

3. Why is playing such an important practice during childhood development?

4. Why are video games such a popular form of entertainment for the digital generation?

5. If school leadership is not on board with the idea of using digital games to teach students, then how would you persuade these leaders to see gaming's potential?

6. Why is failure such an important lesson for students to learn? How does a video game teach failure?

7. What potential gaming platforms are there to use in the classroom? What will be the advantages and disadvantages of using each gaming platform?

8. What is the difference between the role of a teacher and the role of a facilitator?

9. What types of stigma are associated with video gameplay? Is this stigma warranted?

10. What is the difference between formative and summative assessments? How can digital games be used to enhance or provide both formative and summative assessments?

11. Soft skills are defined as personal attributes that describe an individual's ability to interact with others. What are some of the soft skills digital games cultivate in players?

12. What are the skills people need nowadays to thrive in the workplace? How can digital games assist learners to develop these skills?

13. What barriers exist that could hinder the adoption of DGBL? How would you suggest breaking down these adoption barriers?

14. What are the differences between teaching and testing games? How do facilitators use each during classroom instruction and assessment?

References and Resources

AppBrain. (2014). *Top 10 Google Play categories.* Accessed at www
.appbrain.com/stats/android-market-app-categories on January 9,
2015.

Beavis, C. (2012). Video games in the classroom: Developing digital
literacies. *Practically Primary, 17*(1). Accessed at www.alea.edu
.au/documents/item/355 on January 9, 2015.

Blanchard, O. (2010). 10 things Julius Caesar could have taught us
about business, marketing, leadership (and even social media)
[Web log post]. Accessed at https://thebrandbuilder.wordpress
.com/2010/05/20/10-things-julius-caesar-could-have-taught-us
-about-business-marketing-leadership-and-even-social-media on
February 16, 2015.

Blikstein, P. (2013). Seymour Papert's legacy: Thinking about
learning, and learning about thinking. *Transformative Learning
Technologies Lab.* Accessed at https://tltl.stanford.edu/content
/seymour-papert-s-legacy-thinking-about-learning-and-learning
-about-thinking on January 9, 2015.

Carpenter, K., Pager, D., & Labrecque, R. (2013, August). *Teachley:
Addimal Adventure—Bridging research and technology to help
children foster strategy development, conceptual understanding, and
number fact fluency* [White paper]. Accessed at www.teachley
.com/assets/docs/White-Paper-Addimal-Adventure.pdf on
January 9, 2015.

Carpenter, S. K., Pashler, H., Cepeda, N. J., & Alvarez, D. (2007). Applying the principles of testing and spacing to classroom learning. In D. S. McNamara & J. G. Trafton (Eds.), *Proceedings of the 29th Annual Cognitive Science Society* (p. 19). Nashville, TN: Cognitive Science Society.

Chou, Y. (2013). *Top 10 marketing gamification cases you won't forget.* Accessed at www.yukaichou.com/gamification-examples/top-10 -marketing-gamification-cases-remember/#.VOI9zbDF-4Q on February 16, 2015.

Derosier, M. (2014). Game-based social skills assessments: Making the play for better emotional health. *EmergingEdTech.* Accessed at www.emergingedtech.com/2014/07/game-based-social-skills -assessments on January 9, 2015.

Diele, O. (2013). 2013 State of online gaming report. *Spilgames.* Accessed at http://auth-83051f68-ec6c-44e0-afe5-bd8902acff57 .cdn.spilcloud.com/v1/archives/1384952861.25_State_of _Gaming_2013_US_FINAL.pdf on January 9, 2015.

Entertainment Software Association. (2014). *Games: Improving education.* Accessed at www.theesa.com/wp-content /uploads/2014/11/Games_Improving_Education-11.4.pdf on February 16, 2015.

Fishman, B., Riconscente, M., Snider, R., Tsai, T., & Plass, J. (2014). *Empowering educators: Supporting student progress in the classroom with digital games.* Ann Arbor: University of Michigan. Accessed at http://gamesandlearning.umich.edu/wp-content/uploads /2014/11/A-GAMES-Part-I_A-National-Survey.pdf on January 13, 2015.

Games for Change. (2015). *About.* Accessed at www.gamesforchange .org/about on January 23, 2015.

Hearn, M., & Winner, M. C. (2013). *Teach math with the Wii: Engage your K–7 students through gaming technology.* Eugene, OR: International Society for Technology in Education.

Huang, T., & Plass, J. L. (2009). *Microsoft research: History of play in education*. New York: Games for Learning Institute. Accessed at http://g4li.org/wp-content/uploads/2009/10/6-History-of-Play .pdf on January 13, 2015.

Institute of Play. (2014). *GlassLab*. Accessed at www.instituteofplay .org/work/projects/glasslab on January 9, 2015.

Kane, A., & Meyers, G. (2010). Virtual pig: Pfizer's animal health 3-D serious game. *The eLearning Guild*. Accessed at www .elearningguild.com/olf/olfarchives/index.cfm?id=712& action=viewonly on February 16, 2015.

Kapp, K. (2013). *Testing games vs. teaching games*. Accessed at http:// karlkapp.com/testing-games-vs-teaching-games on January 9, 2015.

Korbey, H. (2014, June 9). Surprising insights: How teachers use games in the classroom [Web log post]. Accessed at http://blogs .kqed.org/mindshift/2014/06/surprising-insights-how-teachers -use-games-in-the-classroom on January 9, 2015.

Lenhart, A., Kahne, J., Middaugh, E., Macgill, A., Evans, C., & Vitak, J. (2008). *Teens, video games and civics*. Washington, DC: Pew Research Center's Internet and American Life Project. Accessed at www.pewinternet.org/2008/09/16/teens-video-games -and-civics on January 13, 2015.

Malhoit, L. (2012, August 28). Cisco Aspire game helps CCNA training [Web log post]. *TechRepublic*. Accessed at www .techrepublic.com/blog/career-management/cisco-aspire-game -helps-ccna-training on February 16, 2015.

MindShift. (2014, November 12). A third grader's plea for more game-based learning [Web log post]. Accessed at http://blogs .kqed.org/mindshift/2014/11/a-third-graders-plea-for-more -game-based-learning on January 13, 2015.

National Governors Association Center for Best Practices & Council of Chief State School Officers. (2010a). *Common Core State Standards for English language arts and literacy in history/social studies, science, and technical subjects.* Washington, DC: Authors. Accessed at www.corestandards.org/assets/CCSSI_ELA %20Standards.pdf on February 24, 2015.

National Governors Association Center for Best Practices & Council of Chief State School Officers. (2010b). *Common Core State Standards for mathematics.* Washington, DC: Authors. Accessed at www.corestandards.org/assets/CCSSI_Math%20Standards.pdf on February 24, 2015.

NPD Group. (2011). *The video game industry is adding 2–17-year-old gamers at a rate higher than that age group's population growth.* Accessed at www.afjv.com/news/233_kids-and-gaming-2011.htm on February 16, 2015.

Rideout, V. (2013). Zero to eight: Children's media use in America 2013—A Common Sense research study. *Common Sense Media.* Accessed at www.commonsensemedia.org/file/zero-to-eight -2013pdf-0/download on January 9, 2015.

Robertson, A. (2014). "Angry Birds Stella" launches to increase series' 2 billion downloads. *Forbes.* Accessed at www.forbes.com/sites /andyrobertson/2014/09/04/angry-birds-stella-hands-on-review on February 16, 2015.

Sandford, R., Ulicsak, M., Facer, K., & Rudd, T. (2006). Teaching with games: Using commercial off-the-shelf computer games in formal education. *EA Futurelab.* Accessed at http://archive .futurelab.org.uk/resources/documents/project_reports/teaching _with_games/TWG_report.pdf on February 16, 2015.

Schaaf, R. (2014, March 27). 10 free online educational game sites [Web log post]. Accessed at http://blogs.kqed.org/mindshift /2014/03/10-free-online-educational-game-sites on January 9, 2017.

Schaaf, R., & Mohan, N. (2014). *Making school a game worth playing: Digital games in the classroom.* Thousand Oaks, CA: Corwin Press.

Shapiro, J., Salen, K., Schwartz, K., & Darvasi, P. (2014). MindShift guide to digital games and learning [Web log post]. Accessed at www.kqed.org/assets/pdf/news/MindShift -GuidetoDigitalGamesandLearning.pdf on January 9, 2015.

Shute, V., & Ventura, J. (2013). Stealth assessment: Measuring and supporting learning in video games. *MacArthur Foundation.* Accessed at http://mitpress.mit.edu/books/stealth-assessment on February 16, 2015.

Statistica. (2014a). *Number of apps available in leading app stores as of July 2014.* Accessed at www.statista.com/statistics/276623 /number-of-apps-available-in-leading-app-stores on January 9, 2015.

Statistica. (2014b). *Most popular Apple App Store categories in September 2014, by share of available apps.* Accessed at www .statista.com/statistics/270291/popular-categories-in-the-app -store/.

Steiner, C. (2014, October 15). *Individualization, failure, and fun: Changing the way we educate students* [Video file]. Accessed at http://tedxtalks.ted.com/video/Individualization-Failure-and-F on January 13, 2015.

Takeuchi, L. M., & Vaala, S. (2014, October). *Level up learning: A national survey on teaching with digital games.* New York: The Joan Ganz Cooney Center at Sesame Workshop. Accessed at www.joanganzcooneycenter.org/wp-content/uploads/2014/10 /jgcc_leveluplearning_final.pdf on January 12, 2015.

Thalheimer, W. (2006, February). *Spacing learning events over time: What the research says.* Accessed at www.leerbeleving.nl/wp -content/uploads/2011/11/Spacing_Learning_Over_Time __March2009v1_.pdf on January 9, 2015.

University of Colorado Denver. (2010, October 10). Video games can be highly effective training tools, study shows: Employees learn more, forget less, master more skills. *ScienceDaily.* Accessed at www.sciencedaily.com/releases/2010/10/101019171854.htm on February 24, 2015.

Solutions for Digital Learner–Centered Classrooms

The *Solutions Series* offers practitioners easy-to-implement recommendations on each book's topic—professional learning communities, digital classrooms, or modern learning. In a short, reader-friendly format, these how-to guides equip K–12 educators with the tools they need to take their school or district to the next level.

Designing Teacher-Student Partnership Classrooms
Meg Ormiston
BKF680

Evaluating and Assessing Tools in the Digital Swamp
Michael Fullan and Katelyn Donnelly
BKF636

From Master Teacher to Master Learner
Will Richardson
BKF679

Creating Purpose-Driven Learning Experiences
William M. Ferriter
BKF691

Implementing Project-Based Learning
Suzie Boss
BKF681

Inspiring Creativity and Innovation in K–12
Douglas Reeves
BKF664

Wait! Your professional development journey doesn't have to end with the last pages of this book.

We realize improving student learning doesn't happen overnight. And your school or district shouldn't be left to puzzle out all the details of this process alone.

No matter where you are on the journey, we're committed to helping you get to the next stage.

Take advantage of everything from **custom workshops** to **keynote presentations** and **interactive web and video conferencing**. We can even help you develop an action plan tailored to fit your specific needs.

Let's get the conversation started.

Call 888.763.9045 today.